The Pledge of Allegiance

by Norman Pearl

illustrated by Matthew Skeens

PICTURE WINDOW BOOKS
Minneapolis, Minnesota

Special thanks to our advisers for their expertise:

Melodie Andrews
Associate Professor of Early American and Women's History
Minnesota State University, Mankato

Susan Kesselring, M.A., Literacy Educator
Rosemount–Apple Valley–Eagan (Minnesota) School District

Editor: Nick Healy
Designer: Abbey Fitzgerald
Page Production: Melissa Kes
Art Director: Nathan Gassman
Associate Managing Editor: Christianne Jones
The illustrations in this book were created digitally.

Picture Window Books
5115 Excelsior Boulevard, Suite 232
Minneapolis, MN 55416
877-845-8392
www.picturewindowbooks.com

Printed in the United States of America.

Library of Congress Cataloging-in-Publication Data
Pearl, Norman.
The Pledge of Allegiance / By Norman Pearl ; illustrated by Matthew Skeens.
p. cm. — (American symbols)
Includes bibliographical references and index.
ISBN-13: 978-1-4048-2644-1 (library binding)
ISBN-10: 1-4048-2644-0 (library binding)
ISBN-13: 978-1-4048-2647-2 (paperback)
ISBN-10: 1-4048-2647-5 (paperback)
1. Bellamy, Francis. Pledge of Allegiance to the Flag—Juvenile literature.
2. Flags—United States—Juvenile literature. 3. Emblems, National—
United States—Juvenile literature. I. Skeens, Matthew, ill. II. Title.
JC346.P42 2007
323.6'50973—dc22   2006027222

0254

Table of Contents

Writing the Pledge 5

A Special Celebration 6

The First Pledge of Allegiance 8

A Popular Pledge 9

Changes to the Pledge 10

Understanding the Pledge 12

The Pledge of Allegiance 18

When Do People Say the Pledge? 19

How to Say the Pledge 20

Pledge and Flag Facts 23

Glossary 23

To Learn More 24

Index 24

My name is Francis Bellamy. I wrote the Pledge of Allegiance. Many American children say this pledge each day at school. They speak the words of the pledge to honor their country's flag. Read on to find out more about the Pledge of Allegiance.

4

Writing the Pledge

I wrote the Pledge of Allegiance on a hot August night in 1892. That year, people celebrated the 400th anniversary of Christopher Columbus sailing to America. At the time, I worked for a magazine in Boston, Massachusetts, called *The Youth's Companion*.

A group called the National Education Association was planning a special event for Columbus Day. I was in charge of the committee putting it all together. I wrote the pledge so students would have something special to say that day.

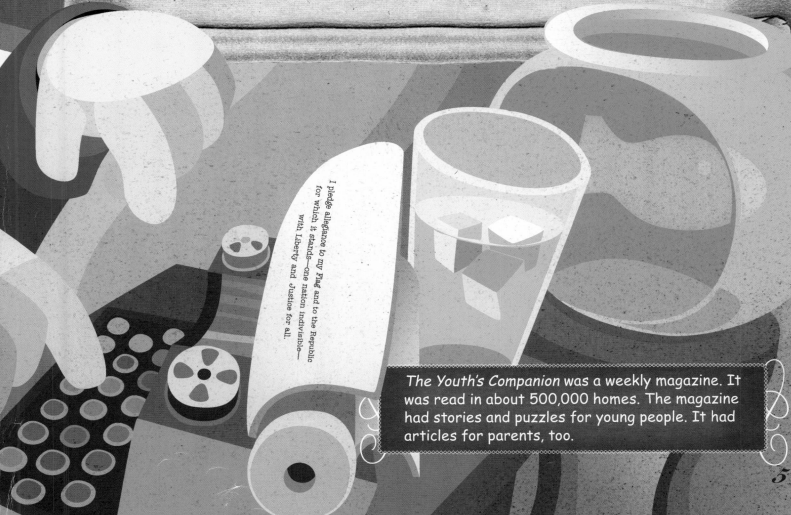

I pledge allegiance to my Flag and to the Republic for which it stands—One nation indivisible—with Liberty and Justice for all.

The Youth's Companion was a weekly magazine. It was read in about 500,000 homes. The magazine had stories and puzzles for young people. It had articles for parents, too.

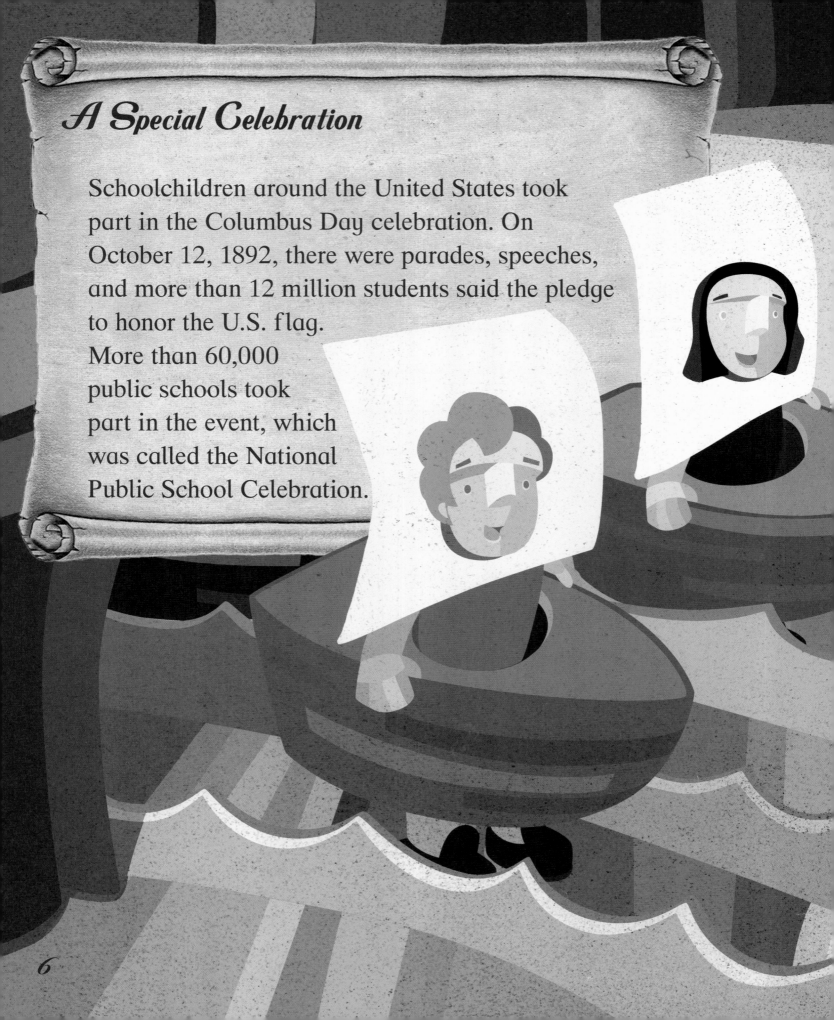

A Special Celebration

Schoolchildren around the United States took part in the Columbus Day celebration. On October 12, 1892, there were parades, speeches, and more than 12 million students said the pledge to honor the U.S. flag. More than 60,000 public schools took part in the event, which was called the National Public School Celebration.

The Pledge of Allegiance was first printed in advance of the National Public School Celebration. The September 8, 1892, issue of *The Youth's Companion* included the text of the pledge.

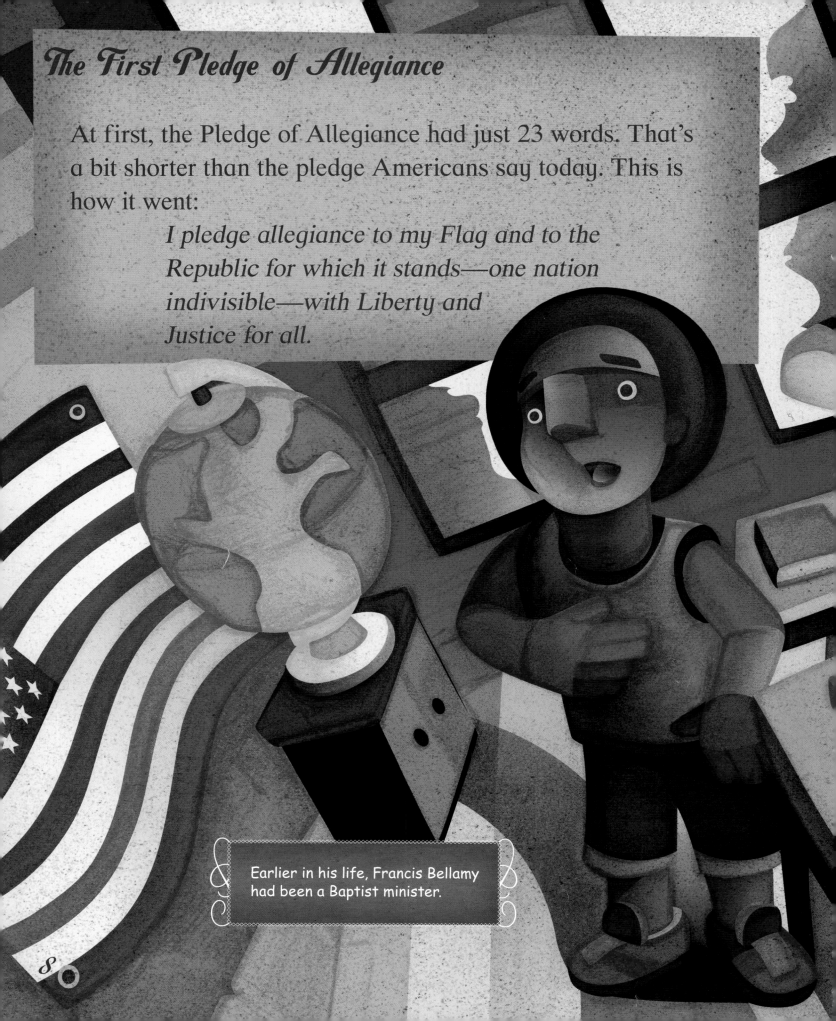

The First Pledge of Allegiance

At first, the Pledge of Allegiance had just 23 words. That's a bit shorter than the pledge Americans say today. This is how it went:

> *I pledge allegiance to my Flag and to the Republic for which it stands—one nation indivisible—with Liberty and Justice for all.*

Earlier in his life, Francis Bellamy had been a Baptist minister.

A Popular Pledge

Right away, Americans liked the Pledge of Allegiance. Saying its words gave them a way to explain how much their country meant to them. Before long, children were reciting the pledge every morning at school. The pledge became an important symbol of patriotism.

Changes to the Pledge

For more than 30 years, people spoke the pledge just as it was written. In the 1920s, there were some changes. People attending the National Flag Conference in Washington, D.C., changed the words *my Flag* to *the Flag of the United States of America.*

The Pledge of Allegiance had become very important to Americans. In 1942, Congress, a branch of the U.S. government, made it the nation's official pledge. Then in 1954, the pledge was changed for the last time. Congress added the words *under God*. This change created the pledge used today.

In 1945, the pledge was given its official title as the Pledge of Allegiance.

Understanding the Pledge

Some students say the Pledge of Allegiance every day in school. But do they know what it really means? Here is a closer look at the pledge and its meaning.

I pledge allegiance to the Flag of the United States of America ...

A pledge is a promise. *Allegiance* means to be loyal or true to something. When people pledge allegiance to a country's flag, they are promising to be loyal to their country.

... and to the Republic for which it stands, ...

A republic is the type of government used in the United States. In a republic, people vote to elect their leaders. No kings or queens rule over the United States. The people rule themselves.

The words *under God* mean different things to different people. Some people think they mean that God has blessed the United States. Other people believe those words mean that the country acts in keeping with God's laws.

When a nation is indivisible, it cannot be divided. This means people in the 50 states join together as one strong nation.

Some people think that the words *under God* should not be in the pledge. They think that in a free country, people have the freedom not to worship God.

... with Liberty and Justice for all.

Liberty means freedom. Americans are proud of the many freedoms they enjoy. *Justice* means fairness. U.S. laws are based on fairness. These laws promise all Americans the same rights.

16

The Pledge of Allegiance

I pledge allegiance to the Flag of the United States of America, and to the Republic for which it stands, one Nation under God, indivisible, with liberty and justice for all.

– U.S. Code

When Do People Say the Pledge?

Classrooms are not the only places where people recite the pledge. The pledge is also said at many official events, such as city council meetings. Veterans groups start their meetings with the pledge. Boy Scout and Girl Scout groups do this, too.

In 1943, the highest court in the United States ruled that public schools could not force students to say the Pledge of Allegiance.

How to Say the Pledge

People stand and face the flag when saying the pledge. They place their right hands over their hearts, too. Unless they are in military uniform, people remove their hats during the pledge. They hold their hats over their hearts as they speak.

Soldiers do not say the Pledge of Allegiance. During the pledge, they face the flag but remain silent. Instead, they give the military salute.

21

Americans recite the Pledge of Allegiance proudly. It is a reminder of their loyalty to the United States. I hope you enjoyed learning more about it.

Pledge and Flag Facts

- In 1923, people at the National Flag Conference changed the words *my flag* to *the flag of the United States*. The next year, they added *of America* after *United States*. They did not want children who came to the country from other lands to think that they were pledging allegiance to their old flag.

- When a flag becomes too worn to use anymore, it should not be thrown in the garbage. An adult should burn it in a respectful manner.

- Massachusetts was the first state to require schoolhouses to have a flag and flagpole. Today every public school in the country flies a flag outside. Some children are taken outdoors to say the Pledge of Allegiance. Other students say the pledge inside their schools.

- When a flag is lowered, no part of it should touch the ground.

Glossary

allegiance — being faithful and true to something or someone

anniversary — the date of an important event

celebration — a party

indivisible — cannot be divided or torn apart

patriotism — love of country

pledge — a serious promise

recite — to say something aloud

reminder — something that causes a person to remember

symbol — an object that stands for something else

veteran — a person who was in the armed forces, such as the army

To Learn More

At the Library

Clack, Barbara. *The Pledge of Allegiance.* Albany, Tex.: Bright Sky Press, 2005.

Martin, Bill Jr. *I Pledge Allegiance.* Cambridge, Mass.: Candlewick, 2004.

Nobleman, Marc Tyler. *The Pledge of Allegiance.* Mankato, Minn.: Capstone Press, 2003.

Ryan, Pam Munoz. *The Flag We Love.* Watertown, Mass.: Charlesbridge, 2006.

On the Web

FactHound offers a safe, fun way to find Web sites related to this book. All of the sites on FactHound have been researched by our staff.

1. Visit *www.facthound.com*
2. Type in this special code: 1404826440
3. Click on the FETCH IT button.

Your trusty FactHound will fetch the best sites for you!

Index

Bellamy, Francis, 4, 8
Boston, Massachusetts, 5
Boy Scouts, 19
changes to pledge, 10, 11, 13, 23
Columbus Day, 5, 6
Congress, 11
first pledge, 6, 8
Girl Scouts, 19
military, 20, 21
National Education Association, 5
National Flag Conference, 10, 23
National Public School Celebration, 6, 7
patriotism, 9
pledge in U.S. Code, 18
students, 5, 6, 9, 12, 19, 23
under God, 11, 14, 15, 18
U.S. Supreme Court, 19
veterans, 19
Youth's Companion, The, 5, 7

Look for all of the books in the American Symbols series:

The Bald Eagle
The Bill of Rights
The Great Seal of the United States
The Liberty Bell
Our American Flag
Our National Anthem
The Pledge of Allegiance
The Statue of Liberty
The U.S. Constitution
The White House